APRIL
PATTERNS, PROJECTS & PLANS

by

Imogene Forte

Incentive Publications, Inc.
Nashville, Tennessee

Illustrated by Gayle Seaberg Harvey
Cover by Susan Eaddy
Edited by Sally Sharpe

ISBN 0-86530-139-5

Table of Contents

PREFACE

April – a month of new life

APRIL...

... A TIME of special days and activities — playing jokes on April Fools' Day; planting trees on Arbor Day; reading books and visiting the library during National Library Week; and decorating, hiding and finding colorful eggs for Easter!

... A TIME of change in weather and surroundings — rain showers are followed by sunny skies and rainbows; birds sing and baby animals are born; flowers blossom and gardens are planted.

All of this and more is the excitement of April waiting to be brought into your "come alive" classroom. Watch students' smiles widen and their eyes brighten as your classroom says "April is here!" from the ceiling to the floor, from windows and doors, from work sheets and activity projects, from stories and books, and especially from you — an enthusiastic, "project planned" teacher.

This little book of APRIL PATTERNS, PROJECTS & PLANS has been put together with tender loving care to help you be prepared to meet every one of the school days in April with special treats, learning projects and fun surprises that will make your students eager to participate in every phase of the daily schedule and look forward to the next day. Best of all, the patterns, projects and plans are ready for quick and easy use and require no elaborate materials and very little advance preparation.

For your convenience, the materials in this book have been organized around four major unit themes. Each of the patterns, projects and plans can be used independently of the unit plan, however, to be just as effective in classrooms in which teachers choose not to use a unit approach. All are planned to complement and enrich adopted curriculum schemes and to meet young children's interests and learning needs.

Major unit themes include:
- April's Arrival
- April Showers Bring Umbrellas, Puddles & Rainbows
- Grow, Garden, Grow!
- Vegetables Everywhere

Each unit includes a major objective and things to do; poster/booklet cover, bulletin board or display; patterns; art and/or an assembly project; reproducible basic skills activities; and book, story and poem suggestions to make the literature connection.

Other topics, special days and events for which patterns, projects and plans have been provided include:

- April Fools' Day (April 1)
- National Library Week (First Week in April)
- Arbor Day (Third Friday in April)
- Easter

APRIL'S ARRIVAL

Major Objective:
Children will develop awareness of the colors, sights, sounds, events and seasonal changes that characterize April.

Things To Do:
- Use the patterns in this book to make decorations for doors, windows, desks, etc.
- Reproduce and use page 24 in observance of April Fools' Day!

- The third Friday in April is Arbor Day. If possible, involve the children in a tree planting ceremony on the school grounds. Garden clubs and conservation groups in most communities are usually happy to supply trees for this purpose!
- Take a walk around the school grounds or a nearby park to identify various trees and their seeds and flowers. Use page 26 as a follow-up activity.

- Reproduce page 23 for each child. Have the children color the page and use it as a booklet cover for their work.

- The bunnies, ducks, chicks and eggs associated with the Easter holiday afford children the opportunity to enjoy these objects as symbols of the miracle of living things. Reproduce pages 28 and 29 in quantities to meet the needs of the class. Instruct the children to follow the directions on page 28 to "find" an Easter basket and to color, cut out and paste the eggs from page 29 in their Easter baskets.
- Send the "letter to parents" (page 10) home to announce the month's activities and to ask for donations for your materials collection. Check your supplies to be sure that you are ready for the month.

To complete the activities in this book, you will need:

crayons & markers	colored chalk	ingredients for recipes
construction paper (assorted colors)	paper plates	(pgs. 63 & 71)
tape	drinking straws	seed catalogs
paste	straight pins	gardening magazines
scissors	tempera paint	bulbs, seeds, seed
stapler	yarn	packets, vegetables,
pencils	tag board	soil, flowerpots &
drawing paper	box	other "gardening"
paper lunch sacks	paper cups	materials
cotton balls	materials for science	
tissue paper	experiments (pg. 54)	

Dear Parents,

Spring is finally here, and that means that our classroom is "bursting" with excitement!

April is a month of celebration, exploration and discovery. During the days and weeks ahead we will be celebrating April's special days — April Fools' Day, National Library Week, Easter, etc. We also will be "celebrating April" by studying and learning about trees, flowers, spring animals, rain, puddles, rainbows, vegetables, gardens and other springtime wonders.

Your child will be involved in special projects and experiments and will bring home many things to share with you. Help your child continue "exploration" and "discovery" at home by showing interest in these projects and activities and by asking questions and making observations.

If you would like to help with our monthly projects, you can collect and contribute paper sacks, gardening magazines, flower bulbs, and lots of seeds and seed packets. Anything you would like to contribute or do to enhance our April celebration and study would be greatly appreciated!

Sincerely,

APRIL ALPHABET

A ... April showers bring May flowers
B ... Buttercups, buttercups everywhere
C ... Candy eggs to hide and find
D ... Digging in the dirt
E ... Easter bunnies and baby chicks
F ... Falling raindrops
G ... Gardens to plan and plant
H ... Happy Easter!
I ... It's springtime!
J ... Jokes and fun on April Fools' Day
K ... Kittens to play with and cuddle
L ... Lilies and lilacs
M ... May flowers are on the way
N ... National Library Week (first week in April)
O ... Open umbrellas on rainy days
P ... Puddles to play in
Q ... Quiet spring mornings
R ... Raindrops, rainstorms and rainbows
S ... Singing birds
T ... Trees to plant on Arbor Day (third Friday in April)
U ... Umbrella — a handy thing to have!
V ... Vegetables to grow and eat
W ... World Health Day (April 7)
X ... X-tra hours of sunlight
Y ... Yellow flowers by the roadside
Z ... Zucchini aplenty!

APRIL

Sunday	Monday	Tuesday	Wednesday	Thursday	Friday	Saturday

HOW TO USE THE APRIL CALENDAR

Use the calendar to:

... find on what day of the week the first day of April falls
... count the number of days in April
... find the number on the calendar which represents April
... mark the birthdays of "April babies" in your room
... mark special days

- April Fools' Day (April 1)
- National Library Week (First week in April)
- World Health Day (April 7)
- Arbor Day (Third Friday in April)
- Easter
- etc.

CALENDAR
ART

APRIL MANAGEMENT CHART

CLASSROOM HELPERS

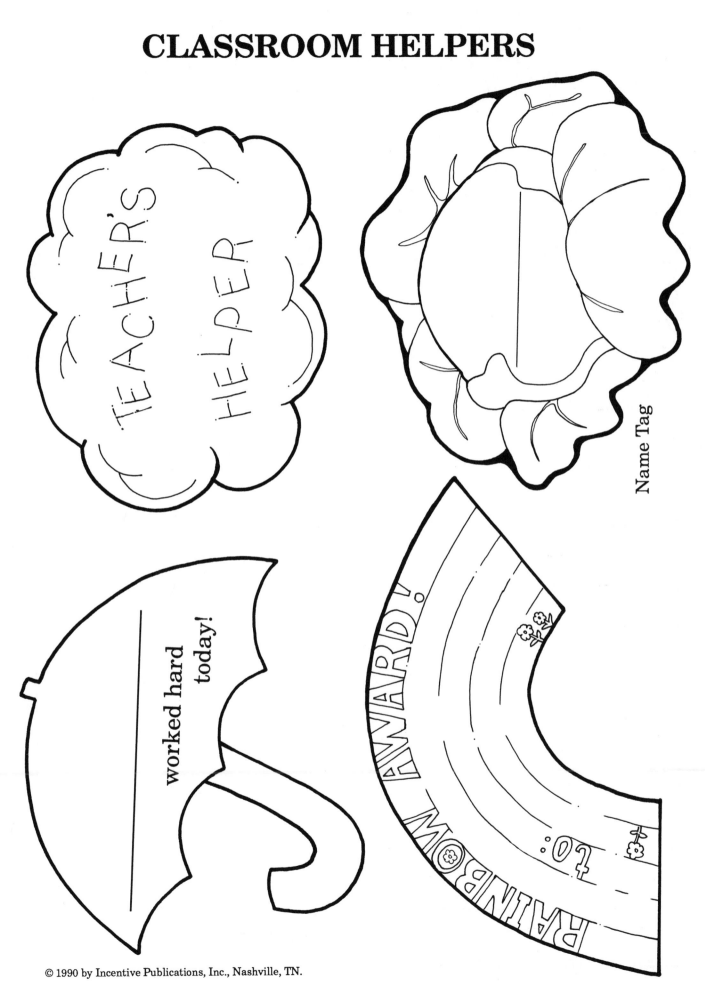

TEACHER'S HELPER

Name Tag

worked hard today!

RAINBOW AWARD! to:

APRIL DOORKNOB DECORATION

Color and cut out this doorknob decoration.
Hang it on your door to say that spring is finally here!

We're Celebrating sunny days

HERE'S WHAT'S HAPPENING IN OUR CLASSROOM

Week of

_____

MONDAY _____

TUESDAY _____

WEDNESDAY _____

THURSDAY _____

FRIDAY _____

SPRING HEADBAND

1. Cut out the "Spring is here!" headband and paste it on a strip of construction paper sized to fit the child's head.
2. Fasten the headband with a paper clip.

© 1990 by Incentive Publications, Inc., Nashville, TN.

19

APRIL BULLETIN
BOARD BORDERS

Accordion fold paper strips to match the size of the pattern.
Tape or trace the pattern onto paper and cut.
Be sure the dotted lines touch the edges.

WAYS TO USE THE APRIL BULLETIN BOARD BORDERS

RAINBOW SHOW-OFF

To "show off" good work, help the children color and cut out rainbow show-offs to attach to their papers. Show-offs make attractive bulletin board displays and great "take homes"!

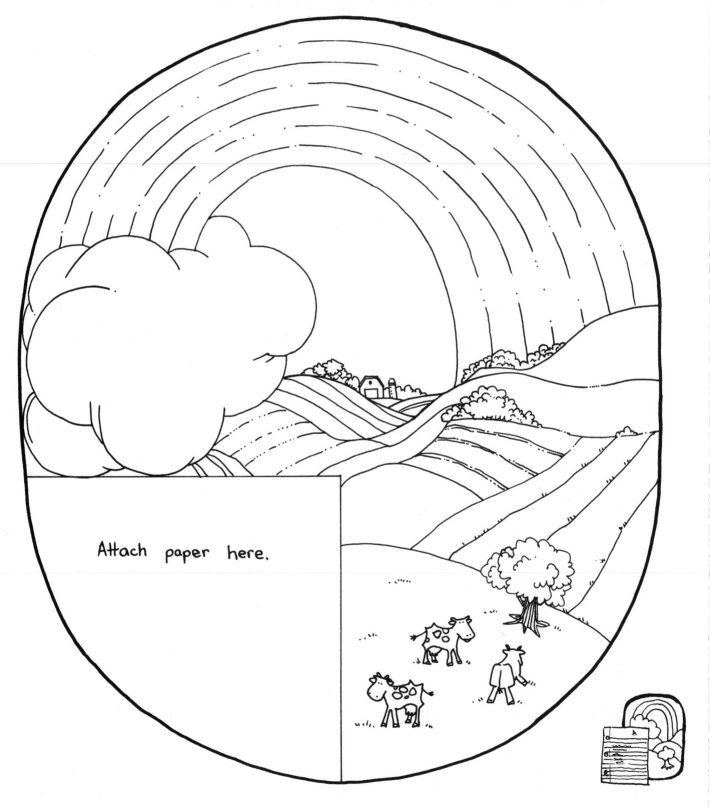

Attach paper here.

In April's Sweet Month,
When the leaves 'gin to spring,
Little lambs skip like farries
And birds build and sing.

MOTHER GOOSE

Name _____

Name _____

AN APRIL FOOLS' DAY PICNIC

What a funny, mixed-up picnic!
Color everything in the picture except the mistakes.
Make an X on 10 funny, mixed-up things.

Finding mistakes
© 1990 by Incentive Publications, Inc., Nashville, TN.

MARK YOUR FAVORITE BOOKS TO CELEBRATE LIBRARY WEEK!

This book belongs to

_____

I ♡ TO READ!

HOME SWEET HOME

An owl, a bluebird, a squirrel, a chipmunk or even a hornet might make its home in this tree.

Draw a picture of the animal and its home that you think might live in this tree.

Visualizing

EGGS ALIKE

Two eggs in each row are exactly alike.
Color the eggs that are alike red and blue.
Color the egg that is different green.

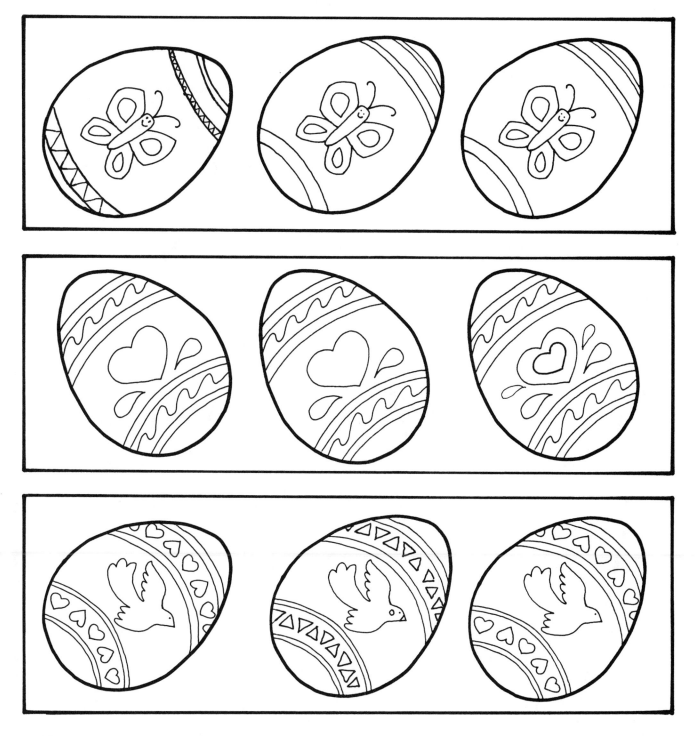

Visual discrimination/following directions
© 1990 by Incentive Publications, Inc., Nashville, TN.

AN ABC BASKET

Connect the letters from A to Z to find a bunny's surprise.

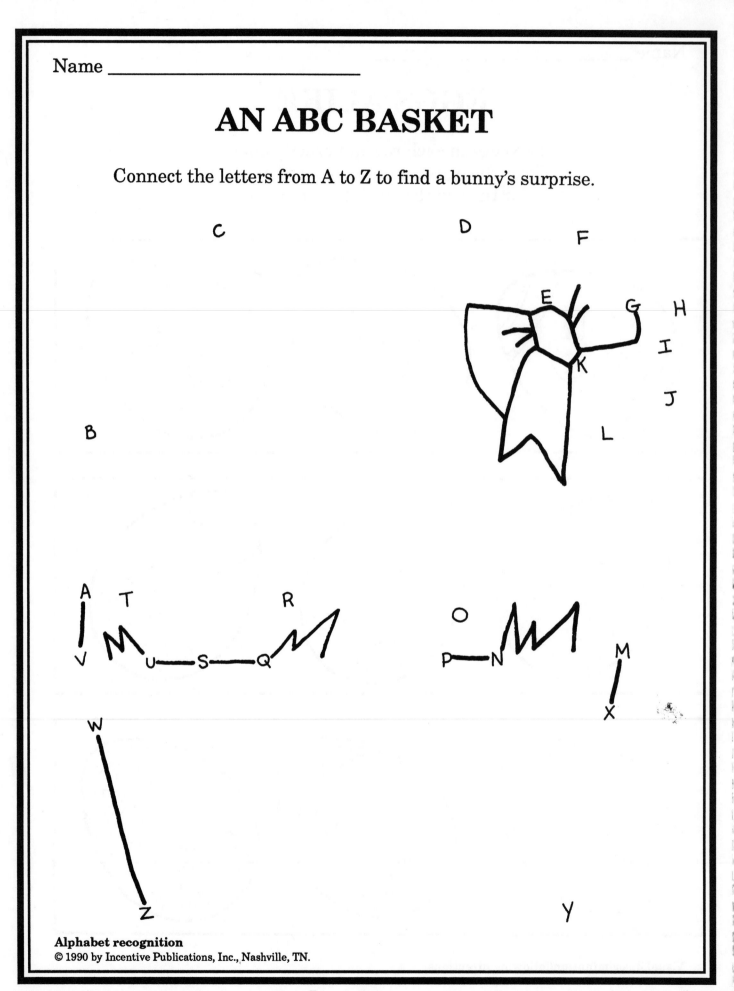

Alphabet recognition
© 1990 by Incentive Publications, Inc., Nashville, TN.

EGGS FOR YOUR BASKET

Use all of your favorite colors to color the Easter eggs below.
Cut out the eggs and paste them in the Easter basket (page 28).

Cutting & pasting/motor skills

© 1990 by Incentive Publications, Inc., Nashville, TN.

FOUR FUNNY BUNNIES

1) PAPER BAG BUNNY BASKET

What To Use:
brown paper lunch bags
construction paper
scissors
paste
markers

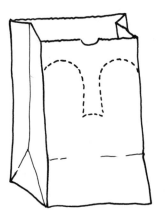

What To Do:
1. Help the children draw "bunny ears" on a flat paper sack and cut around the tops of the ears as shown.
2. Have the children cut ears, eyes and whiskers out of construction paper and paste the features on their paper bags.

Note: The paper bag bunny can serve as a basket for Easter eggs or as a container for a small gift!

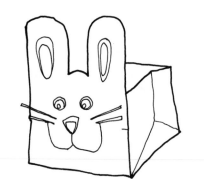

2) COTTON BALL OR TISSUE PAPER BUNNY

What To Use:
construction paper   scissors
paste   colored chalk
cotton balls or tissue paper

What To Do:

1. Reproduce the bunny pattern on page 33 for each child.
2. Have each child cut a bunny out of construction paper and paste cotton balls or crumpled pieces of tissue paper on the bunny to cover it. (Hint: Pull the cotton balls apart before pasting them on the bunny!)
3. Have the children use colored chalk to draw mouths, noses and eyes on their bunnies.

Note: These bunnies make interesting additions to the "April Showers Bring May Flowers" bulletin board (page 39).

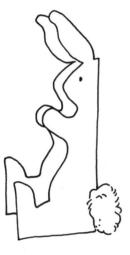

3) STAND-UP BUNNY

What To Use:
white construction paper
cotton balls
pink construction paper
scissors
markers
paste

What To Do:

1. Reproduce the bunny pattern on page 34 for each child.
2. Have each child place a bunny pattern on a folded sheet of white construction paper and cut around the pattern. (Be sure to place the pattern against the fold!)
3. Direct the children to "stand up" their bunnies and paste the "hands" together as shown.
4. Help the children cut "inside ears" out of pink construction paper and paste them on their bunnies.
5. Each child may paste a cotton ball tail on his or her bunny and draw facial features with markers.

4) PAPER PLATE BUNNY FACES

What To Use:

white paper plates
white, pink, black & light blue
   construction paper

scissors
plastic drinking straws
paste

What To Do:

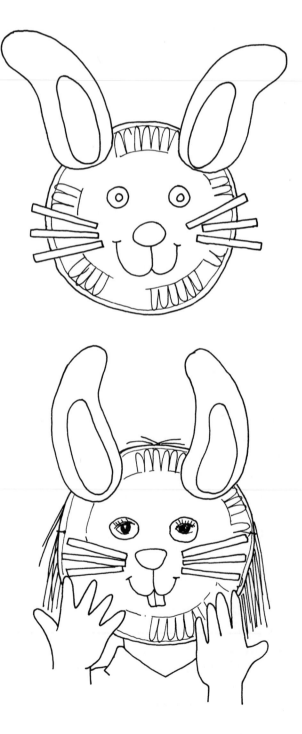

1. Have each child cut two circles out of blue construction paper (for eyes) and two smaller circles out of black construction paper (for pupils). Ask the children to paste the black circles on the blue circles to make eyes.
2. Have each child use the pattern on page 34 to cut two ears out of white construction paper. Instruct the children to color the insides of the ears pink.
3. Help each child cut three drinking straws in half to make whiskers. (Or, use strips of white paper for whiskers.)
4. Have the children cut round noses out of pink construction paper.
5. Direct the children to paste their "bunny features" on white paper plates to make bunny faces!

Note: To make a bunny mask, simply cut eye holes, punch holes in both sides of the paper plate and tie yarn through the holes. Slit the paper plate up to the nose so that the mask will "curve around" the child's face.

32

BUNNY

HALF BUNNY & EAR

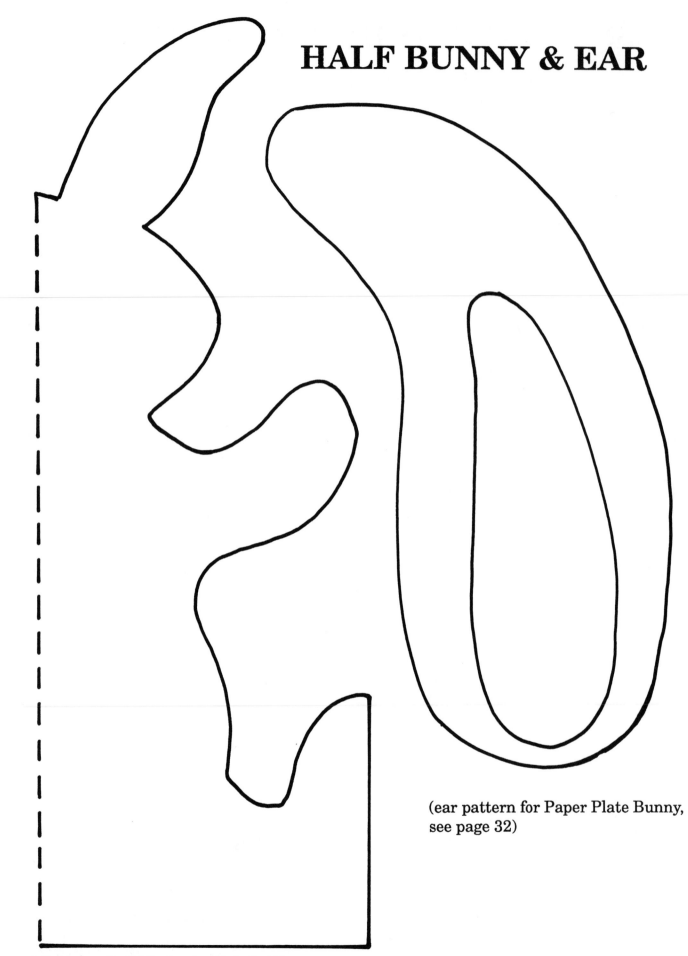

(ear pattern for Paper Plate Bunny, see page 32)

APRIL SHOWERS BRING UMBRELLAS, PUDDLES AND RAINBOWS

Major Objective:

Children will develop awareness of spring showers and of the effects of rain on growing things and daily life.

Things To Do:

- After a rainstorm, take the class outside to examine a puddle! Use bottles, jars and a scoop to collect puddle water. Ask the children to look for living things in the puddle. Scoop some water into a jar and have the children observe how the sediment settles to the bottom of the jar. Take a jar of puddle water back to the classroom for continued observation. Compare the puddle water to tap water. Leave the jar uncovered and have the children check it each day to note how the sludge settles to the bottom.

- Show the children how to make their own rainbows! Take the class outside on a sunny day. Stand with your back to the sun and spray a fine mist from a garden hose in front of you. Have the children stand behind you and look into the spray at a 45 degree angle. The children may not always see a rainbow, but they will have fun trying!

- Paint rainy day pictures. Have the children sprinkle two or more colors of dry tempera paint on sheets of drawing paper. Then ask the children to take their papers outside (remember, it must be raining!). After a few minutes, have the children pick up their papers and "move them around" to spread the wet paint and make designs. Place the rainy day pictures on newspaper to dry.

- Use the poem "Paddle Little Ducks" (page 53) as a finger play. Reproduce the poem for each child and have the children take the poem home to share with family members.

35

Construction:

1. Cover the board with blue paper.
2. Enlarge the duck and umbrella on page 37. Cut the umbrella out of red paper, the duck's body out of white or yellow paper, and the duck's feet and bill out of orange paper.
3. Cut the caption "A Walk In The Rain" out of construction paper.
4. Have the children cut raindrops and clouds out of construction paper (patterns on page 38).
5. Assemble the board as shown.
6. Help the children "curl" strips of white or yellow paper around pencils and paste the strips on the duck to make "fluff."

Use:

Use the board as motivation for language activities and games such as these:

- Begin a story in this way: "One rainy morning in April, Downy Duck decided to take a walk. She picked up her umbrella and headed out the door. Just as she left her own front yard...." Ask the children to take turns adding "segments" to the story. Continue in this manner until a child adds a surprise ending, or add a lively ending of your own.
- Have the children sit in a circle. Begin by saying: "Downy Duck is going to Denver (or Denmark, Detroit, etc.) and he will take a hundred dollars." The first child in the circle must repeat what you said and add another item. The game continues in this manner until all of the children have added an item. More mature children can add items in alphabetical or numerical sequence or limit items to specific categories.

DUCK & UMBRELLA

RAINDROPS AND CLOUDS

Construction:

1. Cover the board with blue construction paper or butcher paper.
2. Enlarge the banner on page 40 and color it with markers.
3. Reproduce the patterns on pages 38 and 40-42 and cut them out of construction paper.
4. Cut green grass out of construction paper (hint: "fringe" strips of green construction paper).
5. Assemble the board as shown above.
6. Display the children's drawings on the board.

Note: See the simple directions on page 43 for adapting this board to celebrate National Library Week (first week in April).

APRIL SHOWERS
BRING MAY FLOWERS BANNER

BUTTERCUP & TULIP

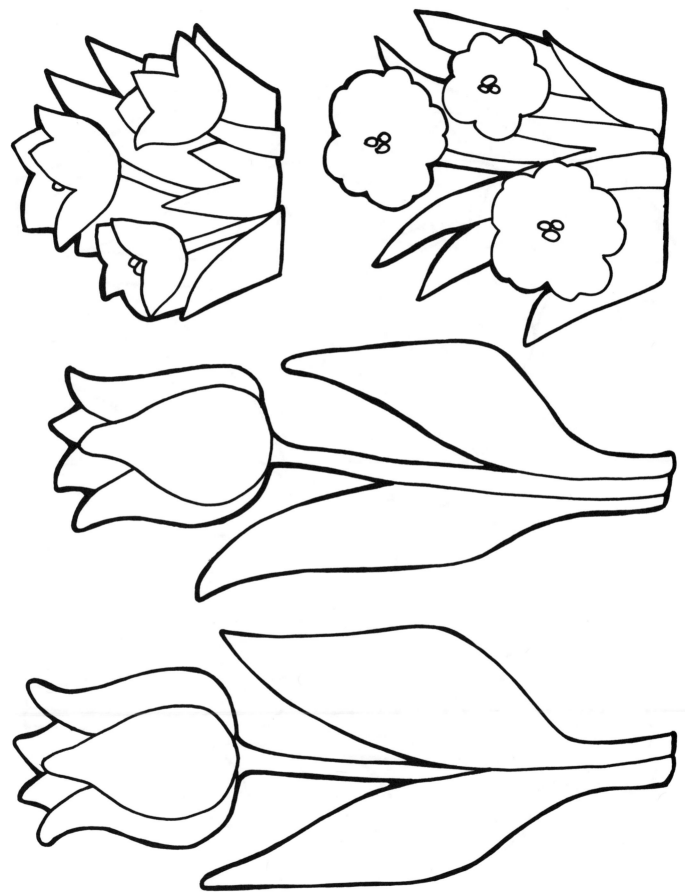

HYACINTH & DAISY

Quick-Change Construction:

1. Enlarge the banner on page 44 and color it with markers. Substitute this banner for the "April Showers Bring May Flowers" banner.

2. Reproduce the duck and umbrella on page 37 and the rainbow and pot of gold on page 45. Cut the patterns out of construction paper and add them to the board as shown.

3. Fill the pot with book jackets and attach a book jacket or construction paper "book" in the duck's hands as shown.

4. Display book jackets of favorite books and/or children's illustrations of characters and scenes from favorite books on the board.

APRIL SHOWERS
BRING TIME TO READ BANNER

cut apart
then rejoin here.

APRIL SHOWERS BRING

TIME TO READ!

'S AND

RAINBOW & POT OF GOLD

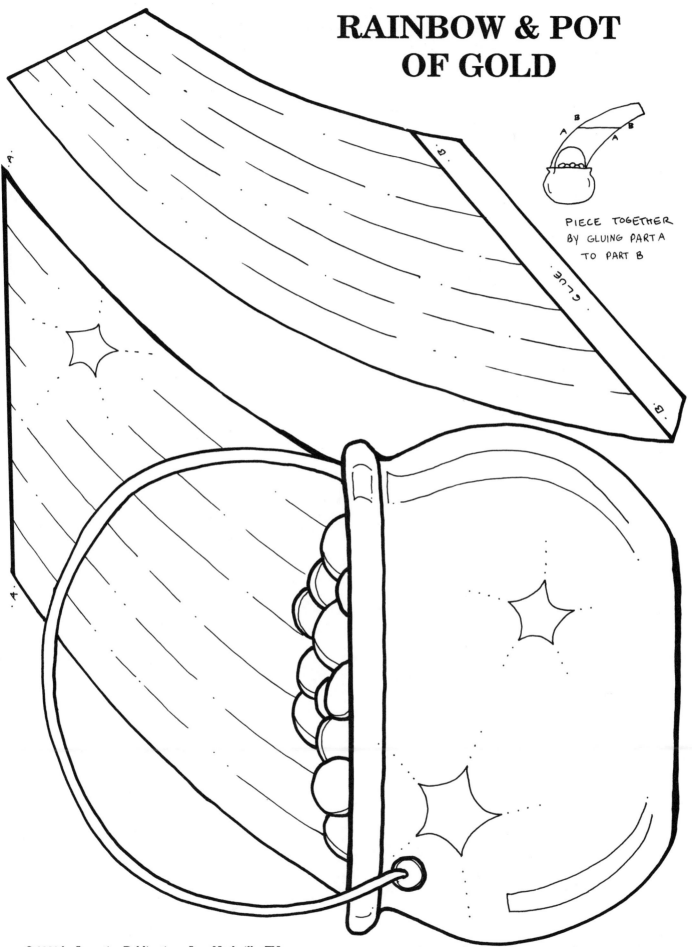

PIECE TOGETHER
BY GLUING PART A
TO PART B

APRIL SHOWERS

Name _____

RAINBOW COLORS

When the sun shines after a rain shower, a rainbow sometimes forms.
A rainbow has seven colors.
Color this rainbow.

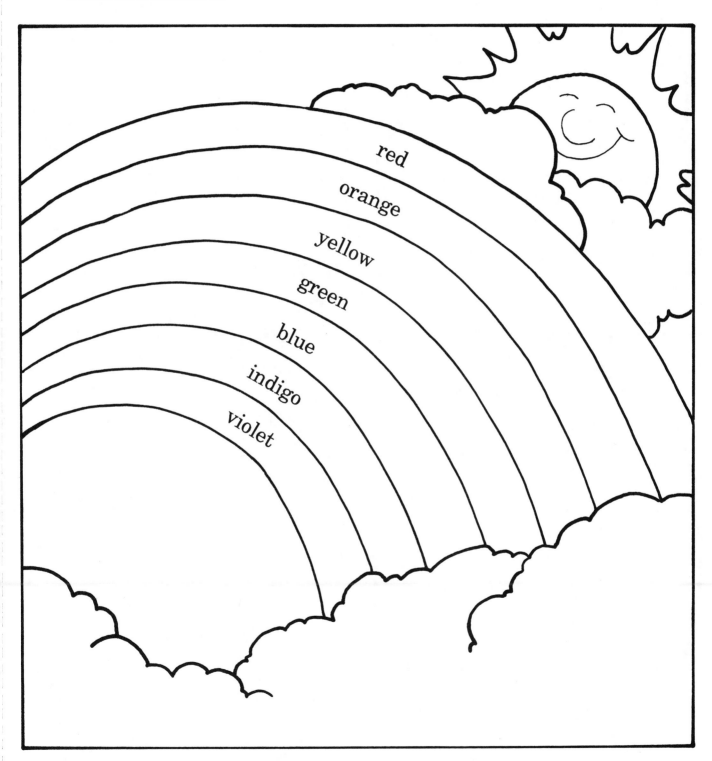

red

orange

yellow

green

blue

indigo

violet

Learning about colors of the rainbow
© 1990 by Incentive Publications, Inc., Nashville, TN.

RAINY DAY RHYMES

Color and cut out the rainy day rhymes below.
Paste them on a sheet of blue construction paper to make a rainy day
rhyme poster.

IT'S RAINING, IT'S POURING

Trace a path to help each bunny get out of the rain.

Solving a maze/visual discrimination
© 1990 by Incentive Publications, Inc., Nashville, TN.

Name _____

Rain, rain, go away. Come again another day. Little birdies want to play!

Find and color 4 birds hiding from the rain.

Finding hidden pictures/visual discrimination
© 1990 by Incentive Publications, Inc., Nashville, TN.

Name _____

RAIN ON THE GREEN GRASS AND RAIN ON THE TREE.
RAIN ON THE HOUSETOP BUT NOT ON ME!

Draw dot-to-dot from 1 to 15 to
find out why it's not raining
on the _____ .
(Animal Name)

Numeral recognition
© 1990 by Incentive Publications, Inc., Nashville, TN.

Name _____

COLOR BY NUMBER

Follow the color key below to color the picture.

1 = red   3 = orange
2 = yellow   4 = blue

Recognizing colors and color words

PADDLE LITTLE DUCKS

(A Finger Play)

Paddle little ducks,
Paddle, paddle all day;
Paddle little ducks,
Paddle, paddle away.

Five little ducks paddling to shore,
One paddled away, then there were four;
Four little ducks paddling toward me,
One paddled away, then there were three;
Three little ducks paddling toward you,
One paddled away, then there were two;
Two little ducks paddling in the sun,
One paddled away, then there was one;
It paddled away, then there was none!

Paddle little ducks,
Paddle, paddle all day;
Paddle little ducks,
Paddle, paddle away.

SIMPLE
SCIENCE EXPERIMENTS

Make A Cloud In A Jar

What To Use:
1 qt. glass jar
hot water
ice cube
flash light

What To Do:
1. Pour 1 cup of hot water in a 1 qt. glass jar. Let it stand for a few minutes.
2. Darken the room and place an ice cube over the mouth of the bottle.
3. Hold the bottle in front of a flash light (very close to the light) and observe the formation of a cloud within the bottle.

Measure The Rain

What To Use:
gallon jar with wide "mouth"
pint jar
red nail polish

What To Do:
1. Fill a gallon jar with 1 inch of water.
2. Pour the water into a pint jar.
3. Use red nail polish to mark the height of the water on the pint jar. Measure the height of the water and make a second mark this distance above the first mark. Empty the jar.
4. Divide the space between the two red marks into ten equal parts by measuring and marking the parts. Then divide the space between the bottom red mark and the bottom of the jar into ten equal parts. Each mark will show one-tenth of an inch of rain.
5. Use the gallon jar to collect rainwater. Pour the rainwater into the pint jar to measure the amount of rainfall.

GROW, GARDEN, GROW!

Major Objective:
Children will develop awareness of and appreciation for gardens and the various stages of plant growth.

Things To Do:

- April is the perfect time to study gardens and growing things! Place seed catalogs and gardening magazines on a reading table. Have the children cut out pictures of plants that grow well in their neighborhoods. Add the pictures to a collage or bulletin board.

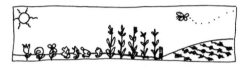

- Explain that plants can be grown from seeds, cuttings and bulbs. Show the children tulip, hyacinth and/or jonquil bulbs and let the children feel the bulbs. Ask this question: "Can you believe that a plant with beautiful blossoms will grow from this dried-up bulb?" Then show an onion and explain that onions are bulbs, too. (Show an onion that is sprouting to demonstrate how the onion bulb sends out new sprouts and to allow the children to observe more rapid growth.) Display pictures of flowering plants and growing onion plants. Let the children help plant the bulbs in pots of soil and add the pots to a windowsill garden (see pages 57 and 58).

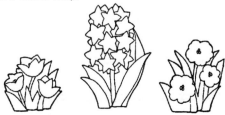

- Take a field trip to a plant nursery. Arrange for someone to guide the children through the nursery and to explain the stages of plant growth. If a field trip is not possible, invite a resource person to visit the classroom!

- Read The Carrot Seed by Ruth Krauss (see page 78). Share the pictures with the children as you read. Then ask the children to "dance" the story!

- The units "Grow, Garden, Grow!" and "Vegetables Everywhere" have overlapping concepts and activities so that the units may supplement and reinforce each other. The division of the units was made to afford clarity of objectives and ease in presentation. In some instances, however, it may be more effective to combine the units and present the projects in a different sequence.

- To make the literature connection, read *In A Spring Garden* (see page 78).

PAPER CUP GARDENS

What To Use:

soil

paper cups

seeds (lettuce, radish, string
    or lima bean seeds are good
    for quick sprouting

construction paper

yarn or ribbon

crayons & markers

What To Do:

1. Have each child decorate a paper cup using construction paper and/or crayons and markers. The children may tie yarn or ribbon around their cups for the "finishing touch."

2. Help each child fill a paper cup with soil and plant a few seeds in the cup.

3. Plant two or three additional cups of seeds to use in a class experiment. Place one cup in a dark place to show the children what happens when plants do not receive sunlight. Do not water another cup of seeds to show what happens when plants do not receive enough water.

4. As the seeds sprout and the plants begin to grow, discuss the growth with the class. Let the children examine the leaves and stems through a magnifying glass.

5. Discuss the differences in the growth of the children's plants and the growth (or lack of growth) of the plants not receiving sunlight and water.

6. At the appropriate time, let the children take their plants home as Easter or "springtime" gifts. The children may choose to replace their plants in larger pots or the yard!

GROW MR. MCGREGOR'S GARDEN IN YOUR CLASSROOM

- Read the all-time favorite *Peter Rabbit* by Beatrix Potter (see page 78). Have a follow-up discussion and allow the children to pantomime how the various characters felt in the story.

- Provide a head of lettuce and carrot sticks for a touching/tasting party! Ask the children to think of descriptive words for two lists — words that describe lettuce and words that describe carrots. Write each list on a chart and keep the charts in the room for reference during the vegetable study to follow (see page 67). Reproduce the lettuce and carrot patterns (pages 59 and 60) and use them to highlight the charts. The patterns also may be reproduced for the children to color, cut out and take home.

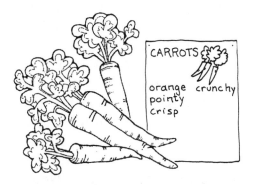

- Grow carrots in a dish and a pot! First, cut off several carrot tops, leaving about half an inch of carrot on each "top." Place the carrot tops in a shallow dish of water and add a few pebbles to keep the carrots from touching. Place the dish on a windowsill (or other sunny spot) and have the children observe daily to watch the carrot tops grow.

On the day when the carrot tops are first placed in water, help the children plant carrot seeds in a pot of soil. Read the directions on the seed packet to the children. Place the pot on the windowsill beside the carrot tops and compare the growth of the plants daily.

Provide a piece of blotter paper, a sponge, a pot of soil and a packet of lettuce seeds. Ask the children to help prepare three lettuce gardens. First, plant several lettuce seeds in a pot of soil after reading the seed packet directions aloud. Then, place a sponge and a piece of blotter paper in two shallow glass dishes, each containing a thin layer of water. Place several lettuce seeds on the sponge and blotter paper. (Note: It is important to use glass dishes so that the roots can be observed during the "sprouting" stage.) Place each of the three containers on the windowsill beside the carrot seeds and wait for the gardens to grow!

Use the lettuce and carrot patterns on pages 59 and 60 to make observation booklets to place beside the gardens. Cut "lettuce booklet covers" out of green paper and "carrot booklet covers" out of orange paper (make a front and back cover for each booklet). Cut 10 to 12 oval shapes out of white paper (following the pattern design) for each booklet and staple or tape the booklets together.

Paste lettuce and carrot seed packets on the appropriate covers and title the booklets: "Our Lettuce Gardens" and "Our Carrot Gardens." Have each child begin his or her "observation records" by writing the dates on which the seeds were planted in the appropriate booklets. Help the children write and/or draw pictures to record the growth of the plants. Keep the children's booklets on the windowsill beside the gardens for daily reference.

LETTUCE

CARROTS

GARDEN TOOLS

Color the pictures of 4 tools that are used for gardening.

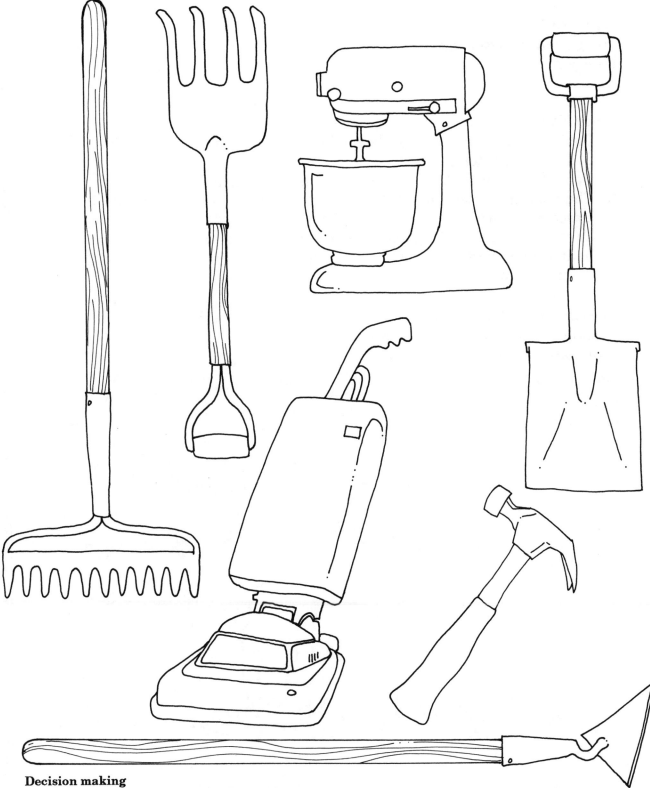

Decision making

SPROUT A SALAD
IN YOUR CLOSET

Children will enjoy participating in this "sprouting" experiment and will have fun tasting and describing the "results"!

What To Use:
mung beans or soybeans
large jar
water

What To Do:
1. Put some mung beans or soybeans in a large jar. (You can find these at health food stores.)
2. Cover the beans with water and let them soak overnight.
3. The next day, drain the water and place the jar in a dry, warm, dark closet or cabinet.
4. Take the jar out of the closet two or three times a day and rinse the beans with cold water. (Note: Do this gently in order to avoid disturbing the sprouts that are forming.)

The children will be amazed at the changes taking place daily. Help them to observe changes in size, texture and color and to notice new shoots. The sprouts should be ready to eat in a few days!

BEANS, BEANS, BEANS

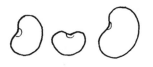

Read the story *Jack And The Beanstalk* (pages 64 and 65). Then have the children draw pictures of the giant beanstalk that Jack climbed.

Ask the children to bring beans from home for sharing time. Try to gather as many kinds of beans as possible to acquaint the children with a wide variety of plants.

Bring a crock pot to class and cook dried beans for the children to "observe" and eat! Explain that the beans are dried in this manner so that they can be saved for later use. This is a good time to discuss world hunger. Explain that dried beans, corn and rice make up a large part of the diet of people in underprivileged countries. Discuss the need for wise use of the earth's produce and each individual's responsibility not to waste food or other natural resources. The most impressive part of this project will be the observation that two cups of dried beans equals a whole pot of table-ready food!

Crock Pot Beans

What To Use:

2 cups dried beans	onion
water	bacon (or cooking oil)
salt	crock pot
pepper	paper cups
plastic forks	

What To Do:
1. Wash the beans and soak them in water overnight.
2. The next day, cover the beans with water and add a slice of onion and a few slices of bacon (or one tablespoon of cooking oil).
3. Start cooking the beans early in the day on low heat. Take the top off the pot at regular intervals to observe the changes taking place as the beans cook. Discuss steam and the process of "softening" the beans. Cook the beans approximately 3 hours or until tender.
4. Taste the beans before serving and add salt and pepper if desired.

Serve the beans in paper cups with squares of corn bread (optional) — umm, umm good!

JACK AND THE BEANSTALK

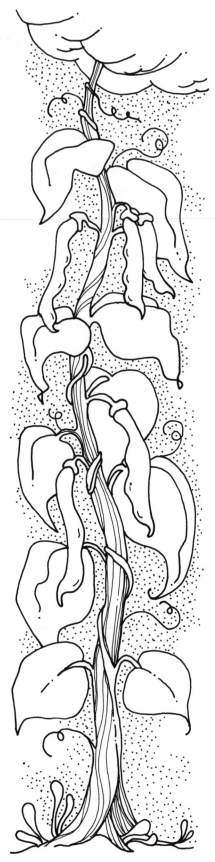

Many years ago a poor widow lived in a shack with her son, Jack. One day she said to Jack, "You must take our cow to town and sell it for money to buy food."

Jack set off to town and soon met a man who offered him a handful of magic beans in exchange for the cow. Jack gladly took the beans and ran home to show his mother what a good trade he had made.

Jack's mother was very disappointed. In her despair she threw the magic beans out the window.

When Jack awoke the next morning, he saw a giant beanstalk growing straight up into the sky. He immediately climbed out the window and up the beanstalk.

At the top of the beanstalk he saw a huge castle. He knocked at the door and was greeted by a giant's wife. She gave him food to eat, but she told him to eat quickly and run away before the giant returned.

Just then, Jack heard the giant roar: "Fe, fi, foe, fum, I smell the blood of an Englishman! Be he alive or be he dead, I'll grind his bones to make my bread!" Jack quickly found a safe hiding place. The giant sat down to eat.

After he had eaten, the giant called for his magic hen. "Lay, hen, lay a golden egg!" he commanded.

As Jack watched, he remembered that the magic hen rightfully belonged to his mother. He had been told that a magic hen had been stolen from his family long ago by a cruel giant.

The giant soon fell asleep and began to snore. Jack jumped from his hiding place and snatched the hen. Then he climbed down the beanstalk to safety.

Early the next morning Jack climbed up the beanstalk again. This time the wife refused to let him in the castle. Jack hid nearby until her back was turned, and then he slipped into the castle and hid. Soon he heard the giant roar loudly: "Fe, fi, foe, fum, I smell the blood of an Englishman! Be he alive or be he dead, I'll grind his bones to make my bread!"

"Husband, you smell this grand dinner that I've made," said the good wife. "Come, eat!"

So, the giant ate. Then he called for his magic harp, which had also been stolen from the rightful owners. "Play, magic harp, play," he commanded. Soon he fell fast asleep.

Jack jumped from his hiding place, grabbed the harp and started down the beanstalk. About halfway down, the harp began to sing out, "Master, Master, I have been stolen!" The giant was awakened and he immediately climbed down the beanstalk after Jack.

Jack jumped to the ground just a step or two ahead of the giant. He quickly grabbed an ax and chopped down the beanstalk. The giant was so heavy that he fell and made a great hole in the ground through which he disappeared forever.

Jack and his mother had recovered the magic hen which laid golden eggs, the bags full of silver and gold, and the magic harp which made beautiful music. They never had to be hungry again, and they were able to do much good for their friends.

WE PLANTED A GARDEN AT SCHOOL ONE DAY

Sung to the tune of *Mary Had A Little Lamb.*

We planted a garden at school one day,
School one day, school one day,
We planted a garden at school one day,
Just to watch it grow.

We planted some lettuce seeds on a sponge,
On a sponge, on a sponge,
We planted some lettuce seeds on a sponge,
Just to watch it grow.

We planted some carrot tops in a dish,
In a dish, in a dish,
We planted some carrot tops in a dish,
Just to watch it grow.

Repeat the first verse.

Note: The children may add their own verses as additions are made to the classroom garden!

VEGETABLES TO GROW AND EAT

Major Objective:

Children will gain understanding of the importance of vegetables to human beings, will become familiar with the physical characteristics of many vegetables, and will learn that plants are living things requiring water and sunlight.

Things To Do:

- Bring a selection of vegetables to class. After discussing the vegetables, have the children touch, smell, shake, taste and examine the vegetables.

- Have the class play "Vegetable Question Box." Write questions on strips of paper such as: "Which is larger, a cucumber or a watermelon?" Place the questions in a box. Divide the class into two teams. Have the teams take turns sending one child to the center of a circle in which you sit holding the question box. After the child draws a question, read the question and ask the child to respond. If the child answers correctly, he or she scores one point for the team. The team with the highest score wins.

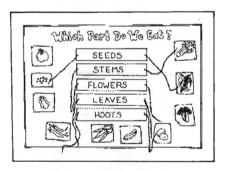

- Construct the bulletin board on page 69 and have the children complete the manipulative activity in their free time.

- Provide seed catalogs, magazines, construction paper, markers, paste and yarn. Help each child label five sheets of construction paper as follows:

  vegetables with roots to eat
  vegetables with stems to eat
  vegetables with leaves to eat
  vegetables with seeds to eat
  vegetables with flowers to eat

  Instruct the children to cut out pictures of vegetables and to paste them on the appropriate pages. Have the children decorate "cover sheets," punch holes in their pages and tie them together with yarn.

- Reproduce and cut out the story starters on page 68. Paste the story starters on tag board strips and place the strips in a basket. Have a child draw a story starter from the basket, and ask each child to add a sentence to the story. Call on one child to end the story — the ending must include the name of at least one vegetable.

Tommy ordered some seeds from a seed catalog. He planted the seeds and two weeks later...

The old man in the little house on the corner grew a garden on his windowsill. One day he saw a funny-looking plant with big red leaves growing in one of his pots...

© 2000 by Incentive Publications, Inc., Nashville, TN.

STORY STARTERS

Sally's mother said, "We have no potatoes for dinner. What will we have instead?"

The old man in the little house on the corner grew a garden on his windowsill. One day he saw a funny-looking plant with big red leaves growing in one of his pots...

Mary thought her Father was joking when he told her they were going to visit a magic garden. Can you imagine her surprise when...

Tommy ordered some seeds from a seed catalog. He planted the seeds and two weeks later...

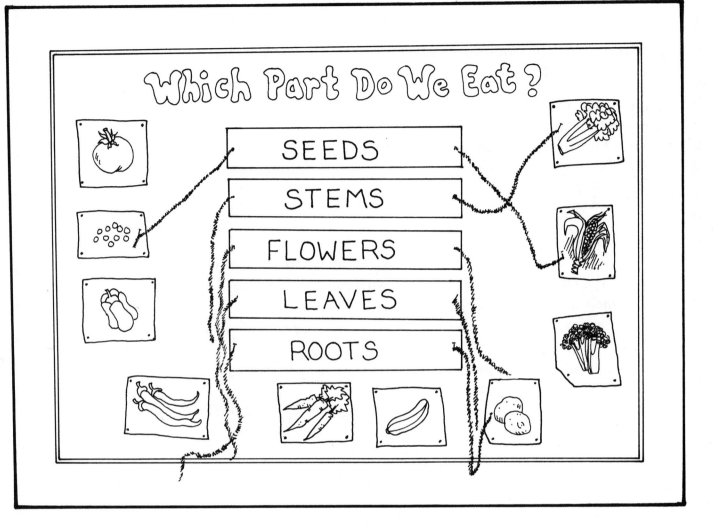

Construction:

1. Write each of the following words on a strip of tagboard: seeds, stems, flowers, leaves, roots. Attach several pieces of brightly colored yarn to each strip.
2. Have the children cut pictures of vegetables out of magazines and seed catalogs and pin them around the edges of the board.
3. Cut the caption "Which Part Do We Eat?" out of construction paper.
4. Assemble the board as shown.
5. Have the children match the words and pictures by pinning the strands of yarn to the correct pictures. (Provide straight pins or tacks.)

POTATO HEAD PLANTER

Children will enjoy making this unusual planter and watching their very own plants sprout and grow!

What To Use:

firm potato with pointed end
   (one for each child — ask
   the children to bring these
   from home)
blunt-point paring knives

soil
seeds
thumbtacks
pipe cleaners
construction paper

What To Do:

1. Help each child scoop out the top of a potato, leaving a one-half inch thick shell.
2. Have the children fill their potatoes with soil and plant seeds in the potatoes.
3. Let each child give his or her potato a "face" using thumbtacks for eyes and construction paper for other features. Pipe cleaners make fun "tails" or mustaches!

SOUP'S ON!

Read the story *Stone Soup* by Marcia Brown (Macmillan) and then make your own stone soup!

What To Use:
crock pot or other electric cooker
paring knife
cutting board
large can of tomatoes
bouillon cubes
vegetables (ask each child to bring a vegetable from home)

Note: You may want to bring a few "key" vegetables in case the children's contributions fail to yield a balanced "soup pot."

What To Do:
1. Assemble the ingredients and utensils on a table.
2. Have the children wash and prepare the vegetables. Your assistance will be needed in cutting the vegetables into small pieces of approximately the same size.
3. Combine the ingredients. Allow each child to add his or her vegetable contribution to the pot. (Make sure that children who forget to bring vegetables have something to contribute, too.)
4. Add a can of tomatoes and two cans of water.
5. Tell the children that, instead of a smooth stone, you will add "magic cubes" to flavor the soup. (You are adding bouillon cubes — but it's magic to the children.)
6. Let the soup simmer all morning. Take the lid off for "taste tests" periodically. The aroma of the soup will be every bit as exciting as the soup itself. Serve the soup in paper cups with plastic spoons and crackers!

Discuss with the children:
- the effect of the heat on the vegetables
- how cooking the vegetables changes their texture, color, aroma and taste

If possible, prepare a plate of raw vegetables. Have the children compare the raw and cooked vegetables. On another day, bring a wok to class and let the children help to prepare a "stir fry" vegetable dish!

THE GREAT, BIG, ENORMOUS TURNIP SHOE BOX THEATER

Read the favorite fairy tale *The Great, Big, Enormous Turnip* (page 73) to provide the background story for this shoe box theater!

What To Use:

shoe box

crayons & markers

scissors

paste

butcher paper (or shelf paper)

copies of pages 74 & 75

What To Do:

1. Read *The Great, Big, Enormous Turnip* to the class.
2. Reproduce pages 74 and 75 for each child. Have the children color and cut out the story frames.
3. Cut strips of white paper (each the width of a story frame and long enough for all eight frames) for the children. Have the children paste the story frames on the strips in the correct sequence, leaving a little space between each frame.
4. Cut a hole large enough for one story frame in the side of a shoe box and a slit through which the story frame strip may be pulled in each end of the box.

Use:

The children can take turns "pulling" their story frame strips through the shoe box theater as they act out the story. Several children may enjoy working together to act out the various characters.

Note: Pages 74 and 75 also may be reproduced for the children to color, cut out and staple together to make "take home" picture books!

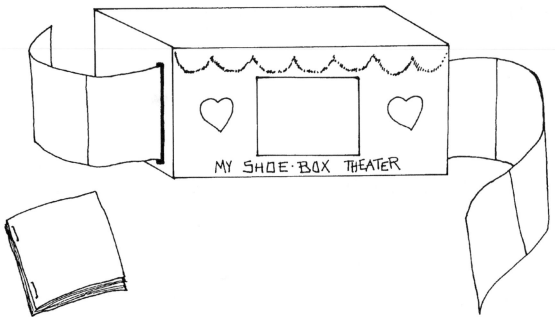

MY SHOE·BOX THEATER

THE GREAT, BIG, ENORMOUS TURNIP

One day an old man planted a tiny turnip seed and then waited for a turnip to grow. Finally, it began to grow – and grow – and grow!

"It's such a big turnip," thought the old man, "that I must pull it from the ground to feed my family."

So, he tried to pull the turnip from the ground, but it was much too big.

"Come help me with this great, big, enormous turnip!" he called to the old lady.

So, the old lady pulled the old man and the old man pulled the turnip, but they could not pull the turnip from the ground.

"Come, child, help us with this great, big, enormous turnip!" the old lady called.

So, the child pulled the old lady, the old lady pulled the old man, and the old man pulled the turnip. Still, the turnip would not budge.

"Here, dog, help us pull this great, big, enormous turnip from the ground!" called the child.

So, the dog pulled the child, the child pulled the old lady, the old lady pulled the old man, and the old man pulled the turnip. Even so, they could not pull the turnip from the ground.

"We need your help, cat!" called the dog.

So, the cat pulled the dog, the dog pulled the child, the child pulled the old lady, the old lady pulled the old man, and the old man pulled the turnip. But, try as they might, they still could not pull the turnip from the ground.

One more time, harder than ever, they all pulled together. And what do you know, up came the great, big, enormous turnip!

THE GREAT, BIG, ENORMOUS TURNIP STORY FRAMES

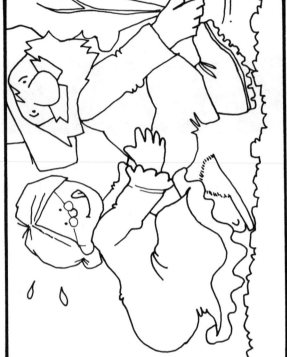

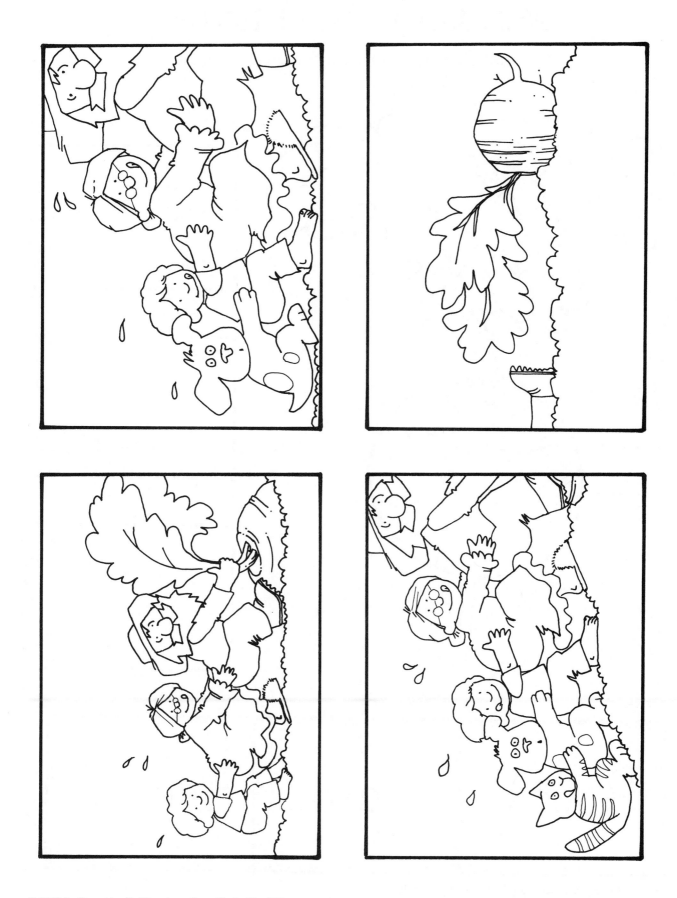

Name _____

ALL ABOUT A TURNIP

Cut and paste the labels in the correct boxes.

Roots | Stems | Leaves

Recognizing & labeling the parts of a turnip
© 1990 by Incentive Publications, Inc., Nashville, TN.

VEGETABLES

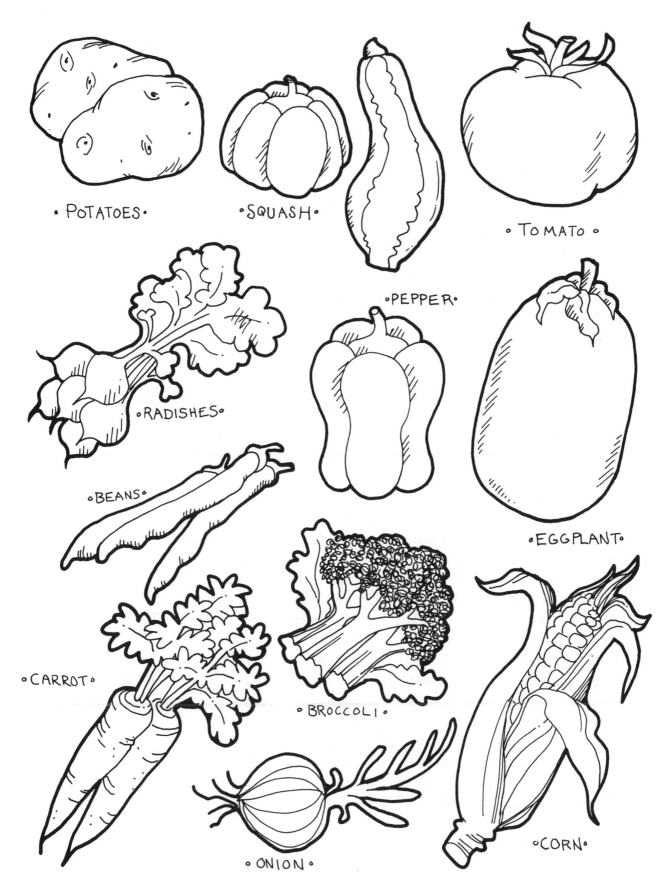

· POTATOES ·

· SQUASH ·

· TOMATO ·

· PEPPER ·

· RADISHES ·

· EGGPLANT ·

· BEANS ·

· CARROT ·

· BROCCOLI ·

· ONION ·

· CORN ·

BIBLIOGRAPHY

All About Mud. Oliver Selfridge. Addison-Wesley.
What mud is, things to do with mud, where to find mud, how to talk about mud and how to write about mud!

April Fools' Day. Dorothy Les Tina. Follett Publishing Co.
How people in many lands enjoy the funniest day of the year, a day that is not a holiday but is still a special time for laughing, jokes and pranks.

Dry Or Wet? Bruce McMillan. Lothrop, Lee & Shepard.
Full-color photographs show happy children enjoying the contrast between wet and dry.

The Easter Egg Artists. Adrienne Adams. Charles Scribners' Sons.
A teacher read-aloud story about a special family of rabbits who paint Easter eggs.

In A Spring Garden. Edited by Richard Lewis. Dial Press.
Short poems about spring's creatures and natural features beautifully illustrated by Ezra Jack Keats.

Once There Was A Tree. Natallia Romanova. Dial Books.
A tree attracts many living creatures, including man. When it's gone, a new tree takes its place and attracts the same creatures who still need it.

Peter Rabbit's Natural Foods Cookbook. Arnold Dobin. Fredrick Warne & Co.
McGregor's scrumptious pureed beets, Flopsy, Mopsy and Cottontail's fresh blueberry cobbler, and Timmy Willie's Sunday scrambled eggs are three of the fun-to-make-and-eat recipes in this collection illustrated by Beatrix Potter.

A Rabbit For Easter. Carol Carrick. Greenwillow Books.
A school rabbit is cared for during Easter vacation by a boy named Paul.

The Rainy Day Book. Imogene Forte. Incentive Publications, Inc.
Rainy day explorations, mud art, raindrop cookies, a rain dance, and rainy day exercises and experiments are just a few of the rainy day, wet weather activities in this little book from the Tabletop Learning Series.

Richenka's Eggs. Patricia Polacco. Philomel Books.
Babushka, who paints eggs, becomes friends with an injured goose who makes miracles.

The Tale Of Peter Rabbit. Beatrix Potter. Warne.
This all-time classic recounting of naughty Peter Rabbit who really didn't mean to get into trouble holds children as spellbound today as it did more than fifty years ago.

A Tree Is Nice. Janice May Udry. Harper & Row.
Delightful illustrations portray the many seasonal delights afforded by a tree —from swinging merrily to raking leaves.

What Makes It Rain? The Story Of A Raindrop. Keith Brandt. Troll Associates.
The characteristics and importance of water are shown as a raindrop journeys through the water cycle.

When The Root Children Wake Up. Helen Dean Fish. Green Tiger Press.
A group of root children wake up to the exciting sights of the new spring season.

Index